Optimus Rhymes

A flat-footed journey

Akshay Upadhyaya

BookLeaf
Publishing

India | USA | UK

Dedication

To my parents—
For your endless love, patience, and belief in me.
This is for all the dreams you nurtured quietly.

Preface

Optimus Rhymes is a collection born not from scholarly pursuit, but from quiet moments in the forest, the hush between distant calls of gibbons, and the untamed rhythm of the wild that surrounds my work as a wildlife biologist. As someone who spends most days observing primates and listening to the language of the trees, poetry felt like a natural extension—an instinctive translation of thoughts that words alone often fail to capture.

This is my first venture into the world of books, and it feels both strange and beautiful to present something so personal. These poems are fragments of my journey—moments of solitude, wonder, uncertainty, and gratitude—woven together in rhyme and reflection. Though inspired by the natural world, they also stem from deeply human emotions, often stirred by memories, people, and quiet observations.

Acknowledgements

Writing *Optimus Rhymes* has been a journey unlike any I've taken before—one that wandered far from research papers and field notes, yet remained deeply rooted in the world I know best.

First and foremost, I express my deepest gratitude to my mother, Sita Devi, whose strength and love have been my greatest anchors. To the memory of my late father, Narayan Upadhyaya, who left us in 2008—your quiet wisdom and gentle spirit continue to guide me in ways I cannot put into words. This book carries a part of you in every line.

To my brother, Alakesh Upadhyaya, and sister-in-law, Pragya Joshi Upadhyaya, thank you for your unwavering support, encouragement, and belief in me—even when I doubted myself. Your presence has been a constant source of strength.

I am also very grateful to BookLeaf Publishing for providing the platform to put out my work.

1. Tell Them I Tell Stories

Tell them I like to tell stories,
All stored as precious gems
In pockets of my memories.
Stories of the voiceless, yet vocal,
Unreal, yet very real.
Tell them I share visuals
Of the roads less travelled,
Where you need no car
Or planes to reach beautiful places—
In the warm, yet cool caress of Mother Nature,
And her evergreen embrace.

2. Scared To Fall Asleep

My dreams are far too sweet
Compared to waking days,
So I hesitate to fall asleep—
They always slip away.
Reality feels heavy,
A bit too undefined,
And I'm just caught somewhere
Between the heart and mind.
I'm scared to fall asleep
'Cause I see old friends again—
Laughing, sharing stories,
Like nothing's ever changed.
I see my father strumming tunes
On warm and golden eves,
My mother by the doorstep,
And my brother full of mischief.
So I'm scared to fall asleep
'Cause those moments feel so near—
A world that's soft and shining,
That somehow draws me clear.

But when I wake, I carry them—
These pieces that still glow.
Not gone, just gently tucked away
In dreams I've come to know.

3. Bharat's Dilemma

Overwhelmed by grief,
The great king breathes his last.
The young prince in Rajgriha
Returns home, as he must.
But to his astonishment,
He finds his kingdom in gloom—
For his father took eternal rest,
Consequent of his mother's boon.
Vexed by her actions,
He refuses to ascend the throne.
Instating his brother's *padukas*,
He rules away from home.
Thus, the young prince performs his duty,
Stationed in Nandigrama,
While he waits for the return
Of his brother—the Lord, Shri Rama.

4. Melancholic Nights

Let's talk about those summer nights,
When the sky wears the veil of dark clouds.
And even after the brightest beginning,
The light eventually fades.

I sit and wonder where the light went,
For I see no twinkling stars.
What used to be a mighty blue canvas
Is now so depressively dark.

Let's talk about those scars
That symbolize our falls—
When our courage left us,
And fear consumed our souls.

Let's revisit the transitions
Our confused hearts once felt—
When our beliefs collapsed,
And we refused to melt.

Oh, I wonder where the light went,
For I see no twinkling stars.
What used to be a mighty blue canvas
Is now so depressively dark.

5. The Gambler

The gambler wore an innocent face,
Played well among the dead—
Gambling with the feelings
Of those held by tiny threads.
Deceptive, sweet words he carried
In his quiver of dark intent,
And he had plenty of friends
Who failed to see what he truly meant.
A happy gambler he strived to be,
Concealed himself in grey—
Disguised as an innocent human,
He preyed on the broken each day.
And so the fools fell—
Those who thought he was a friend.
Pounded by grief, they trembled,
Shaking their heads in the end.
Traumatized, they forfeited
To the gambler's clever game,
And lost their trust forever—
Even in friends who came in their name.

6. Hot And Cold

Your words fly
Like a feather in the wind
So light and fragile
Yet so hard to perceive
Often I wish dead silence
But I am caught off guard
By your constant recurrence
Everyday up on my chat
And it gives me agonizing thoughts
Knowing someone else has your heart
But I wish you find the one
Who actually knows your worth
And distant I wish to be
From these feelings that I hold
Which seem to be thriving everyday
In your presence
Leaving me in between the hot and cold
So let this be a fair goodbye
For I can't be a fool forever
I hope you know that you are loved

So I leave this piece; A reminder.

7. Void

Strolling by the lanes of yesterday,
I revisit the frames,
Voyaging on a sea of empty spaces,
Where float the corpses of my dead wishes.
And hence, I trod further,
Shrouding my agony in laughter,
Towards the shades of pretension,
Hiding myself in crowded detention.
I yearned for words of kindness,
But experienced utter silence.
With all my might,
I packed up my pride
And got on the grumpy ride,
On the road
Where light seemed a lot further.
But I now had a guide:
The dark side, molded
And perceived as the greater light.

8. Hold The Doors Open

I wait, patiently,
As I look for a reason
To hinder my intent
On keeping my word
And to make amends.
I wait, silently,
As dust on the highway struggles to settle
By the force of the fleeting monsoon winds.
But I see no traveller my way,
As I look, ardently,
To hold the doors open.

9. Make An Atheist Pray

They're the cold, dank days
That make me think of you.
Oh Lord! Are you even real?
And do you decide
What a person sees?
Or is this just an illusion?
I know not what faith truly is.
If you are what people say—
Do you think it makes you great,
When our prayers go unanswered
Forever?
Oh Lord, do you have something to say?

10. Dead Leaf Amidst The Green

Oh, what a mess it has been—
Terrible dreams have found
Their home in me.
My insides are falling to the ground,
And I feel like a dead leaf
Amidst the green.
It's been a long time
Since I've felt alive.
I try to recall the sight
Of us running in the wild.
Oh, it's been so long
Since I've felt the same.
And every day feels like a burden.
I try to sleep,
But the nights are getting worse—
Still, I do want to see
The sun shine once again.

11. As Scarred As Me

Often I pause and see,
As the moon whispers your presence to me.
In awe, I gaze and wonder:
What seems so flawless from so far away
Is just as scarred as me.
It hides behind clouds, soft and slow,
Like words I never got to show.
Still it glows, through every phase—
A quiet witness to my silent maze.
And in its light, I feel you near,
A memory blurred, but always clear.
Though distance keeps us worlds apart,
You linger like moonlight on my heart.

12. The Farmer

I wake up a farmer,
And I feel so great;
I tend to my cattle,
And I grow my own bread.
But I know not why
People don't treat me the same—
Not like they treat the rich ones,
Just because they're literate.
They work in offices,
While I work my own land.
I provide them food,
Yet they own the markets.
They wear suits and shoes,
I wear a rugged shirt and an old hat.
They retire and still get paid,
But I work hard my whole life—
And my worn-out feet will tell them that.

13. Of What Things Shall You Think ?

Of what things shall you think
When all the colors begin to fade—
As hopelessness befalls you,
And it matters not
Whether they love or hate?
Of what things shall you think
As you lie there, struggling to breathe,
When absolute nostalgia is all you feel—
For all those summers, and all the falls,
The touch of your beloved, so long gone?
As the emptiness cripples you from the inside,
And you lie there, awaiting your end.

14. False Saints

I try to run away
From everything I believed in,
'Cause none of it has ever been true—
And now it feels like a sin.
So distant I wish to be
From this series of thoughts
That feed me nothing but pain.
They've made me fragile,
And drained my will to speak again.
Trapped in a sea of falsehood,
All my paddles went in vain,
And now I find myself lost—
In a world full of false saints.

15. Why Does It Feel This Way ?

Why does it feel
Like I'm bound
In the hatred of life?
Why am I so entangled
In its web?
This fog of not understanding myself—
What kind of cloud is this?
You strike me every day,
O life,
What kind of punishment is this?
I'm just living,
But I don't know what I'm searching for.
I'm just growing afraid,
Of the feeling of losing myself.
I feel broken,
In this world that feels so meaningless.
People buy happiness with ease,
But sorrow—
It's something that never sells.

16. Should You Find The Rain Too Depressing

Should you find the rain too depressing,
I shall hold you by my side.
For as long as the pain keeps pouring,
I shall be there as your knight.
When darkness comes to veil your shine,
I shall repel it with all my might,
And love you till the very end,
As you fight your demons inside.

17. Storm Whispers

As the thunderstorm rages,
I blankly stare out the pane.
The sound of rain silences my mind,
And for a moment, I breathe again.
But the wind slaps back remembrances,
Long buried by time—
Of the carefree moments,
Back when we used to shine.
The sound of the thunder
Brings tremors to my ears,
Just like the woes of lost love
In an old, broken heart.
The treetops sway,
And the barbets start to cry,
As their nests get blown away
Under an ugly night sky.
But the storm calms down,
The slow silence creeps in.
As the night grows quiet,
I pick up my pen—and begin.

18. Cower

Am I a coward?
For never finding the words
To say that I'd endure every ache
Just to see you smile again.
I don't know how to explain
That no matter the distance,
No matter the silence,
I'd still be here—
Quiet, maybe, but present.
And even when it's hard,
I'd choose to stay,
To stand beside you—
At your highest,
Or when it all falls apart.
I don't need forever.
I just want the truth of now.
You, walking beside me,
Everything else can wait

19. Runaway Silence

We were on a road,
through the woods,
where folks seldom ventured—
until its end.
Where the dense canopies
shielded the moist ground
from the piercing light
of the red-hot sun.
We were on a quest
to get away
from all our woes
and never come back—
trampling on the dead leaves,
just like yesterday's memories.
We took a path that began
past all the known tracks.
We were on a road,
trying to outrun our thoughts
that hindered our being—
until our feet gave way.

We were on a road,
through the woods,
where folks seldom ventured—
and never turned back.

20. If I Could Draw

If I could draw, I would draw all my insecurities,
And all my troubles,
Paste them on my wall,
And count all my struggles.
If I could draw, I would draw people's dreams,
And all of their pain,
The ones which seem
Impossible to restrain.
If I could draw, I would depict all my sins,
Those my heart allows to creep
In the middle of the night,
'Til I slam myself to sleep.

21. Macaque Morning

Up, down, left, right!
I wake to find them all around,
Screeching, jumping, making sound,
Counting each crumb of leftovers found.
Outside the office kitchen, they play,
One young macaque grabs clothes to sway,
Left to dry out in the sun's warm light,
He climbs the rooftop, feeling bright.
To my right, I see a mum,
With her baby, hopping and having fun.
The sandy barren ground beneath,
Life for them is food and fun, a treat.
It's a joy to watch them run,
As they leap and jump beneath the sun.

Greetings Reader!

Thank you so much for reading through to the last page of this collection. Your time and attention mean the world to me. I hope these poems resonated with you at some point, sparked something within, or offered a new perspective. Your support is deeply appreciated, and I am grateful for your journey through these words.